THE LONGING TREE

VIDISHA RAMTEKE

ISBN 979-888530686-7

To mom and dad, my brother and my friends.

Contents

Preface

"Poetry exists in the silence and gaps between words.
It's created on silence, like music. And so what emerges is actually what can't be articulated any other way."
-Meena Alexander

Acknowledgements

It has been 4 years since I first had the urge to express myself with poems. Initially, I published my poems on my Instagram account. From there I met a lot of poets and became a part of the community of writers. I felt at home with them. My first ever collaboration was with Mehul. And it was a great experience.

I am also grateful for my best friend, Sanchay who not just encouraged me but has always been there in the process.

I am very much inspired by the poet, Emily Dickinson whose poems are the home to my soul.

1. Do I fear the stars?

After all the beautiful things,
They stare and leave their impact.
How naive I was to put questions in the universe,
Which was nothing but stardust.
I remember how they spark and light,
I remember how it witnessed our smiles.
I remember that touch in the lone sky,
I remember that wind's whisper,
When we walked the mile.
I was counting on you,
Because it felt my hopes are preserved,
But when the dark sky turned into blue,
In the absence of dusk, I missed you.
When I saw you being broken,
I wondered the heaviness of hope,
You held tight.

It made me afraid how you encouraged
Souls with just mere light.
Because I fear every universe's creation,
Which is too beautiful not to be broken.

2. Timeless now

The stolen stars in that lone night -
With that not so amusing breeze -
It felt pain, until it last -
For its old - own light -
Even in this pause - this stillness -
There are words, underneath my skin -
Can you hold me - for a moment -
Because watching you leave ;
Is itself an eternity to feel -

3. Next time you cry, remember the starry night sky

The slow breeze passed away,
Witnessing the mere observer.
Into the shade of orange and purple,
It reflected silence, utter silence.
With the endless infinity beyond chaos,
The orange sky turned blue.
With the stillness around,
And the mystery of the crowd.
The calmness was found.
Into the pages of fiction,
It felt like a box of illusion.
With the lone essence,
Even the existence felt delusion.
But, as the game is to be played,
The universe holds all the souls together
And into the darkness, bury it like a treasure.
So the next time you cry,
Remember the starry night sky.

4. To colour the universe of my own.

I felt tired with the lows and highs,
With this universe's unreachable skies.
I wondered why they said,
The sky is the limit.

When my only limit was to shatter into pieces.
I have always been the one, who felt stuck.
Uncomfortable with the pleasant noise.
And little by little,

I stopped feeling the connection.
With whatever left was so-called relation.
I wanted to find a way back,
To colour the universe of my own.
Just to hold the courage to speak.
To dance, to laugh, to love.
Just once,
Unapologetically.

With every atom left in my universe
I would simply live,
Without questioning the love,

Of the other being.

5. I am just a human

I'm just a mere observer,
Of this unstable universe.
I'm just a mere seeker,
Of this everlasting serenity.

In a small jar of peace;
Where everyone wants to fill something,
Where thoughts are stuck;
Where silence never reside;

I want to keep it empty.
I want to keep it simple.

I'm just another observer,
Who is not just his thoughts or his moments,
But is eternal at every stage.

Thought change; so do our actions.
Although I seek inseparability,
But, Alas I'm just a human.

6. Death of my hope

Just the ashes remained,
For they say it's a reward.
I feared the fearless,
The invisible, The unknown.
Into the realm of peace,
Far away from the creator,
The home of gravestone was seeked,
Where my hope is not yet buried.
These sounds haunt me at night,
The death of my hope screams,
The tears don't come easy,
And what's left is the silence, we dream.

7. Would you mind taking my verse far away?

If I lend you my ears,
To recite a poem which is my own,
But you're too busy falling in long stories,
That you forgot the phrases which are in the poetry.

And with the metaphors beyond contexts,
You broke them all just to combine them once.

But when I asked you to recite it the way I own,
The bits and pieces would not make them justice.

So, I paused to understand your stories,
Where the characters are known,
The theme is stillness beyond willingness.

Where the world is neither huge nor small.

But enough to grasp, if it falls.
I tried to capture the conversation,
Among the forest, where I took the shed.

Into the journey to your long stories,

I found reasons not to worry.

So after all this time,
If I ask you just a little question.

Would you mind taking my verse far away?
Even knowing that's not certainly your way.

8. Voices in the void

There lie the secrets,
Underneath my skin.

There lie the silences,
Beyond the words that can speak.

For me, the lone stillness subsists,
Which give the warmth of a chaotic breeze
Amid nowhere I seek a home in the abandon
What's left was so surreal to exist.

9. You make me fade away

The daisies got my heart when you hold it,
With the fragrance, you lost within,
you make me fade away,
Into the realm of being.

You are the tale,
I will never get bored to narrate,
You are the poem that my heart knits,
Your words that are left unspoken,
Arc all that I worry about sometimes,

I can no longer stay away from you,
So I will meet you into the silence,
When you look at the bird's chirping,

When you look at how the rain get lost,
When it reaches the land.

When you find the death is not what I fear for,
But the moments which I never lived.

10. Illusion of being lost

Where will you go,
When you feel trapped within yourself-
Whom do you talk with,

When you yourself were collecting the broken pieces'
Why will you cry?

When you are good at faking a smile.
Why will you scream?
When your silence is what defines you.

And at the end,
When you go busy feeling void, tired of being numb-
You will realize, the person you were holding from so long,
Was just an illusion you created in your mind.

11. The paper and you

You carry so much inside yourself,
That even the page awaits,
At the dusk, before you left it unfinished,
It stays wondering when will you be back.

However, whenever you appeared back,
You never ended the incomplete part.
It made the paper wonder,
Your red eyes,

Your unstated words,
And your stillness.
The paper wants to cry,
Watching the existence of yours.

It even asked the pen previously,
But every pen happened to be the guest.
So the paper stop wondering,
And began learning from the one who made him awake. You.
Like after being in a hurricane,

It made you standstill.
After crying, weeping and thinking,

It made you free.
Now every time you become sad,

It doesn't bother the paper anymore.
Because for him,
It knows you're the strongest.
It has ever seen.

12. Back into my heart

Was that a trap or a cage?
Was that silence ever had to be filled?
Was that chaos or a journey?

My mind stuck, my body felt terrified.
Into the shade of orange and yellow,
I felt my heart started beating,
Into the realm of green.

I felt my soul started searching
For the tiny beaming of spark.
Then, for a moment what I did was,
Just took a breath and chased the light.

Not the one, which is too bright to be admired.
But the little ray like a canopy,
That felt me like a pal.

Which rejoiced my weakness,
And admired my solitude.
Which made me wonder,
Into the infinity of leeway

And which dropped me inside,
The void between the woodland.
And taught me how the canopy
Found its way back into my heart.

13. Voyage of life

We all are travellers,
Stuck between moments and memories,
From finding a home to feeling at home,

Through heartbreaks to breathtaking,
Feeling void yet eyes filled
Still finding moments to smile.
We all are travellers,
Meeting new faces yet searching for old,
From laughing so hard to keeping pain on hold,

From making many efforts to being effortless,
To living in paradise, still missing the hell,
We have to find moments to travel.
Because in the end, we all are travellers!!!

14. Stillness to being

Have you ever talked with the wind?
The silence it holds,
The secret it keeps.

The way it helps you, wipe the tears up.
The way it spread colours in your life.
Do you even remember?

The first time it revealed the truth;
That it's not wind, that make the fairies fly.
Do you even remember?

The first time, you told the lie;
And that would have been,
The biggest secret back than.
But that secret is nothing
Less than that the wind keeps.

15. Dreamers in star

I saw you in the sky flying,
But there was some hidden fear behind.
You looked so calm and precious,

Even the wind followed your path.
And all the books you read -
Never forget your fragrance.
And the moments you held my hand,

Makes me feel nothing,
That I can put in words.
Every time you said goodbye,

It felt like you are flying again.
And it makes me feel so proud,
That my love never leaves the sky.

I searched you in all the places,
Wherever you left the little pieces of yours,
And wrote you a letter each day.
Every time I wrote a word,

It felt like holding your hand,

So you can never blame me,
For you never received one.

And this time when you came back,
I smelled freedom which,
Took me away with you,
Forever to your paradise.

16. Bridge in the waves

Let's have a ride in the wonders of my dreams.
I came together with a rainbow yesterday,
Who seized me in the three layers of sky,

Initial was beyond the letters can enlighten any way.
It felt as if I was confronted with the part of my essence,
Which was missed ever since,

But alas it didn't last long,
Probably it was created with better, extraordinarily fallen hearts.
Furthermore, I met with the shooting star
Which was so tangled with the moment

I got on near and implored his desire
He intended to fulfil mine
And mine was to make him free.

And then, later, I greeted
With the pause of my soul,
With the clue that unties my being,

With the serenity of my scream,

With the invisibility of the rainbow,
And with the pureness of the sky.

17. Lost tears

Sometimes I feel as if I am neither moving nor moving on.
An unknown place, from which even the darkness is petrified.
I don't want to stay but I don't want to run either.
I am perplexed with the dilemma that is it real or just a mirage.

I am stuck somewhere or am I nowhere.
What am I? A structure of flesh and bones.
With a heart-pumping pain into my veins.
Then why it is devoid of all the agony?

No feelings, no emotions.
Only a vast emptiness, which expands to the infinite ends of the infinitely enthralling universe.
So many scars on my soul but not a single evidence of their existence.
It's as if I have burned every moment I ever lived.

And it won't be long before I will burn to ashes.
And on that day I will be united with the emptiness inside me.

18. Death is not the destination

The quiet breeze passed my way,
Leaving me into the awe of being alive
I shared the endless silence with the sky
With the infinity of my infinite self
I felt my soul nearest, my body silent
And, my hands touching the universe of my own.
I whispered to the last beam of the dawn
To trap me into the passage of its eternity
And it gradually said the joy is to seek it
TIll the verge of last stardust left in your galaxy
To cherish the end of the fusion
Just to realize the end is where you drown
That be the moment,
Where the essence of breathing
The dreadful life you once felt
Cease when the stars will give you their light,
And, the sound with the vast stillness
Will take you beyond the idea of being alive.

19. Life, beyond the illusion of being.

It's not just a voyage,
Or a glimpse of your reflection.
It's about the bottom of your beauty.
It's about beyond the end of eternity.

It's not just about all the victories,
But also about stillness beneath the fear,
Which drown you and made you lost within.

It's not always about the grief of gravestone,
But questioning the sadness of the loved ones.

It's not just about until when?
Sometimes it's only about "now"
And never again.

20. Journey of gashes to my heart

You came, and I left the exact moment.
And they were sitting there all the time,
Feeling all blue and yet they searched me,
They were waiting for me to be admired.
But I was busy comforting the chaos.
For all the means I have laughed, cried,
Smiled and felt the anguish and the misery.
The Cosmos of there being held the power
To ask a question to my spirit freely.
With the endless Infinity of my soul,
I offered them a silent pause
Which took them beyond the
Illusion of answer and at that
Moment I was the question
And I was the answer itself.

21. And this was the way through

What if, one day I wake up,
Just to find that you are the story,
I always write.

Each day, a little more,
Sometimes the happiest part of it exists,
Which took me to the ocean of joy,

And sometimes to sky full of clouds,
Where my tears are always hidden,
But in the end I find you
In the sky full of stars,

And also in the same ocean
Where these tears couldn't stay,
And I found you were
The paradox of my thoughts.

What if the story of yours,
Would never be completed
But turned out to be the chapter of mine
And this was the way through,

To which I write you a little
And find me the most.

9 798885 306867

Printed by Libri Plureos GmbH in Hamburg, Germany